MY WILDERNESS

An Alaskan Adventure

Claudia McGehee

little bigfoot
an imprint of sasquatch books
seattle, wa

For Jenny and her Alaska boys—
Andy, Ben, and Jim

Copyright © 2015 by Claudia McGehee

Manufactured in China by C&C Offset Printing Co. Ltd. Shenzhen, Guangdong Province, in October 2014

Published by Little Bigfoot, an imprint of Sasquatch Books

20 19 18 17 16 15   9 8 7 6 5 4 3 2 1

Editor: Tegan Tigani
Project editor: Nancy W. Cortelyou
Illustrations: Claudia McGehee
Design: Anna Goldstein

Library of Congress Cataloging-in-Publication Data is available.

ISBN: 978-1-57061-950-2

Sasquatch Books
1904 Third Avenue, Suite 710
Seattle, WA 98101
(206) 467-4300
www.sasquatchbooks.com
custserv@sasquatchbooks.com

Fox Island sits off the coast of Alaska,
one of many islands strung through the waters
like jewels in an emerald necklace.
It is a rugged, wild place.
Otter and seal play on its shorelines.
Eagles hover high above the cliffs.

No one lives on Fox Island anymore.
Stormy weather and tricky ocean currents
make it difficult to reach most of the year.

When I was nine years old, I lived one winter on Fox Island,
with my father, an old trapper named Olson, six blue fox,
a family of angora goats, and Squirlie.

This is what happened.

Father liked to visit snow-covered lands carved out long ago
from the ice and sea. He wanted to paint in Alaska and
asked me if I wished to go. We pleaded with
Mother until she said yes. Squirlie came too.

It was 1918. Alaska was not yet a star on the flag.
It was a time when the world was wide, travel was slow,
and unexpected adventures happened, even to children.

We boarded a train from New York bound for Seattle. A few weeks
later, we stepped off a steamship in Seward, an Alaskan seaport
whose timbered walkways smiled their welcome.

The wilderness is where we wanted to live, but close enough to town to buy supplies now and then. Father borrowed a boat to explore the bay and the nearby islands.

A smudge on the horizon appeared; a man rowed out to us. Mr. Olson was an old frontiersman, gnarled like driftwood, but kindly in face and spirit. Olson lived on Fox Island, not far away. He raised goats and fox there.

"I'll show you the place," Olson shouted out, and we followed him around a bend in the bay.

Like a crouching giant, Fox Island loomed ahead. Its great mountain peaks were covered with evergreens. A dark pebble beach fringed a sheltered cove where our boats landed. Olson pointed to the sky; the first bald eagle I'd ever seen circled above.

Once ashore, Olson introduced us to the other Fox Islanders. Three Angora goats bleated hello. I bleated back. Blue fox darted shyly around a wooden corral.

Olson's tidy log cabin stood off from the beach. Close by, there was an unused shed in need of some fixing up.

It was the perfect spot. The north wind whispered we had found our wilderness home.

From Fox Island, the mainland appeared as just a misty blue outline. Seward was thirteen miles away, but on fair-weather days like that bright September morning, it looked much closer. Olson said it took three or four hours to row there, give or take the winds.

First we cleared the old shed, repairing the floors with planks of sweet-smelling cedar and stuffing thick moss into cracks between the logs on the walls. We put in a new window, two wood stoves, bookshelves, and a platform bed against the wall.

Our cabin felt cozy.

I sland life was simple. Each morning, after chores, Father painted outside. Sometimes I sketched in my notebook with him. Sometimes I helped Olson with his animals. Mostly, I explored.

Squirlie and I hiked the winding trails around the island. Anything could happen in the wilderness. A rustle and snap from deep inside the forest stopped me in my tracks. Was it a grizzly bear? Olson said they sometimes swam to the island. A shadow crossed the trail ahead . . .

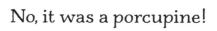

No, it was a porcupine!

On the beach, I collected seashells, smooth stones, bleached bones. A gigantic piece of driftwood became my lookout. Out in the ocean, movement caught my eye. Was that a pirate ship speeding toward us, eager to kidnap a new cabin boy?

No! It was a family of whales, tails
knifing through the water.

I walked back through the forest, the soft bed of leaves and pine needles velveting my steps. Something wet and spongy touched my hand. Was it a wood troll, coming to drag me down to its underworld?

No! It was Billy, one of Olson's goats,
pressing his nose against my palm!

The wilderness made me hungry. When suppertime came, we sat by the fire and ate wonderful meals Father invented. Later in the evenings, Olson often joined us, his blue eyes twinkling as he told tales about panning for gold and fur trapping on the Yukon.

At bedtime, Father played his flute for me, the island's night voices chiming in. Sometimes he read from a storybook, like *Robinson Crusoe* or *Treasure Island*. The wind whistled down the stovepipe as the fire crackled and popped. Soon I was dreaming of shipwrecks and treasure maps.

The days turned gray and colder. It rained and rained. We stayed indoors and filled the cabin with quiet activity. I drew or worked on my math sums while Father sketched or wrote letters. We'd play old-fashioned games, like checkers and chess.

In late October, I tasted my first steely snowflakes. We invented "snow baths," running outside naked, throwing ourselves in soft white snow banks, and then scrubbing down with snow from head to toe. It was only cold for the first instant! Then we raced back inside the cabin and dressed for the day.

I didn't have the right winter boots. Olson had a pair of
ladies' boots he let me borrow. They *were* warm.

On clear days, Father still worked outside, shivering, painting, and then dashing into the warm cabin to thaw his fingers.

I made friends with the cold, tromping the white woods, looking for animal tracks, and digging out snow houses.

I was an otter.

I was a bear.

I was Prince of the Mountain.

King of the Wilderness!

I was a little lonely.

We watched the weather. If it looked fine, we rowed the long route to Seward and stayed for a few days, collecting mail and buying supplies.

Once, on a trip back to Fox Island, the sky turned dark and wild. A terrible storm arose.

Our dory pitched up and down between walls of waves. I clenched my oars tightly and tucked Squirlie deep inside my pocket. Father worked his oars as best as he could. I was frightened our boat would tip over into the churning blackness. Through the driving rain, I caught a faint glimpse of our island. If we missed it, we would be pulled out to sea.

Little by little, we rode the surf into the shelter of the cove. Finally, our dory's bottom dragged against the pebbled beach of Fox Island. Olson was there to help us in.

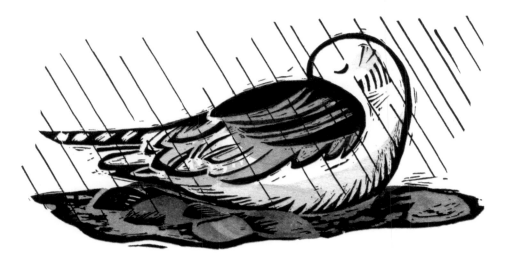

That night, we listened to the gale howling outside our cabin. My legs were still wobbly, and my arms ached from rowing. Squirlie was still afraid. We ate supper quietly. We did not read or draw. We slept close.

The tides ebbed and flowed. Early spring dripped from our cabin's windowsill. The steamer arrived in the bay blowing her whistle. Soon we would go back to New York.

Father packed our trunks and prepared his finished paintings for shipping.

To Seward

Our last day on Fox Island, I sat next to the water's edge, saying good-bye to my wilderness home. I listened to the island so I could remember it better. The waves pulled across the pebbles. The gulls laughed at the sun. The wind whooshed through the tall spruce trees.

I kissed the goats and hugged Olson.

An eagle soared above us, guiding us back to the mainland. We left Fox Island behind, but the wilderness came to stay in my heart forever.

AUTHOR'S NOTE:

My Wilderness is based on a true father-and-son adventure. Nine-year-old Rockwell Kent III (Rocky, to his family) and his father Rockwell Kent II traveled to Alaska in the late summer of 1918. Rocky's father was an up-and-coming painter seeking fresh inspiration. He also wanted to share his love of the wilderness with his eldest son. The pair lived on Fox Island with Lars Olson, an aging frontiersman and the island's sole human inhabitant, for seven months until the spring of 1919.

Rocky and his father wrote many letters to friends and family during their stay. They also kept journals. The elder Kent's written records were published in 1920 in a book called *Wilderness: A Journal of Quiet Adventure in Alaska.* I am indebted to this memoir for helping me better imagine Rocky's daily life on Fox Island. Doug Capra of Seward, Alaska gave me a deeper perspective of the Kents' historic stay. Thanks to Chris Kent, Cecilia Esposito, and Scott Ferris for helping with my research.

Rocky's father made many important paintings while in Alaska. A few months after returning to New York, these paintings were exhibited at a successful art show. Some of Rocky's drawings were shown as well.

Rocky had many other adventures throughout his childhood including bicycling with a school group from Connecticut to Cuba and traveling alone on a passenger liner from France to America. He loved to draw but chose to be a scientist when he grew up.

Later in life, Rocky recalled the months spent on Fox Island as one of the happiest times of his life.

While neither Rocky nor his father ever returned to Fox Island, I'm sure Fox Island remembers them well.

Rockwell Kent II: 1882–1971
Rockwell "Rocky" Kent III: 1909–1986

For further background and resources, please visit Claudia-McGehee.com/MyWilderness.

Rocky outside the Fox Island cabin.

Photo by Rockwell Kent, rights courtesy of Plattsburgh State Art Museum, State University of New York, USA, Rockwell Kent Collection, Bequest of Sally Kent Gordon.

Olson and Rocky, with goats.

Photo by Rockwell Kent, rights courtesy of Plattsburgh State Art Museum, State University of New York, USA, Rockwell Kent Collection, Bequest of Sally Kent Gordon.

Rocky's father, Rockwell Kent, in a hooded fur coat (taken in Greenland, ca. 1930)

Unidentified photographer. Rockwell Kent papers, Archives of American Art, Smithsonian Institution